Life's Many Colors

Life's Many Colors
A Collection of Free Verse Poetry

By

Donna M. Priddy

DORRANCE PUBLISHING CO., INC.
PITTSBURGH, PENNSYLVANIA 15222

ISBN # 0-8059-6866-0
Printed in the United States of America

First Printing

For information or to order additional books, please write:
Dorrance Publishing Co., Inc.
701 Smithfield St.
Third Floor
Pittsburgh, PA 15222
U.S.A.
1-800-788-7654
Or visit our web site and
on-line bookstore at www.dorrancepublishing.com

Dedicated to humanity...
Family...
Friends...
with love and devotion from my heart
2004

Contents

People Need People

As an artist chooses color, we all need one another
Range, variety, we all belong to creativity
Diversity, custom, whatever we all trust in
Nationality, ability... all are connected to one family tree:
Humanity, mixed together, blended well
Yes, this story...life's picture will tell
Each color plays an important part of a masterpiece
All share value regardless of race
For the artist sees beauty in every face
As people need people
Color — this rule of thumb is true
None other applies
Distortions...they lie
Damaging highlights, destroying brother
This picture will darken, leaving life without hue
Expression will lack; the painter stands back, shaking head side
to side
This ugliness is hard to hide
Decision, change, intensity, range
This broad spectrum
To choose from is the best when:
People need people; love does tell
When all color applied, blended well...
The artist satisfied
Creativity, diversity, lend to:
Human expression learn from life's lesson
We all have a voice in the world with language universal
Unity works...
People need people; life's pallet displays
It's array of color accenting objects begotten
This creativity let it be...regardless of what people say
Though some may bend it...some want only to lend it
Others come along, they try to mend it, creating muddy colors
Abstracting, distortions, making change strange with contor-
tions...
Reality blends well; no price will pay; truth never sells...for:
People need people, as you will see; in the world's masterpiece,
there's room for you and me

Music Man
Dedicated to Mr. "V"

Music Man, play if you can...for me
This tune, you see...
For gifted you are, a bright twinkle star in the dark night
You bring delight to all eyes who see
Make music for us to hear, perhaps even to shed a tear
With boldness and delight,
Set our souls to new height of happiness...
Play on, endlessly forever
Life needs you
A healing balm you are...
You will go far in life, you see...
As a full grown tree
Shades us from the powerful sun...
When it burns bright...
As so does life
Play with all your might
Your strength makes others fight...
Yes, joy is contagious,
Though to some you may appear outrageous,
Just let them go in their own gloom
There is no room for them in life you see...
Play on, each song is sung, and when you are done
Memory continues
For each song will linger, forever in our minds...

Moments In Time

Moments in time...
As a flame flickers,
Moments in time
Seem to pass by
Quicker and quicker...
What one does see today will not be again...
It is gone and then;
Only memory holds them...
As the thought goes away,
Moments in time won't stay
Value each of its kind, their messages may never be again
Lost, gone forever, as the waves of the sea never stay...
That hearts may recollect,
Love and respect all those...
Moments in time

Where the Warm Wind Blows

Where the warm wind blows,
It hollows out the sand on a distant shore
Where on some rocks I stand,
I listen as earth speaks to me...
The water's waves forming foaming white peaks...
I look upwards towards the sun; its rays cascade down
Eracing all fears, anxiety's frown
Here, freedom comes to me as it always does...
Where the warm wind blows,
The way I wish life was

As Mighty as the Wind

As mighty as the wind
As tall as the wave
Forces unseen, unruly behave
Repaying the earth for damages done
Disrespect and mirth, silent victory won
Consequence responds with its voice unheard
Displaying its strength, yet no eye may see
All gives way until eternity renews
As mighty as the wind, yet as small as the dew
Mercy restores all those whom…
Pain and destruction laid waste their lives
Vows make change, teaching us to be wise
Unheeded warnings, deliverance ignores
As mighty as the wind…
As the waves come ashore…
Life, in its abundance, repays as it restores
Future has its way, even before it comes
Tapping each on shoulder, warning everyone
Destiny waits, while indecision procrastinates…
As might as the wind,
As still as the small voice…
Whatever decision makes,
Let wisdom rule each choice

Be Yourself

Be yourself
Be strong...
Take courage...it won't be long
Before you will stand and stare in face
All those who scoffed and gave up pace
But you continued to be yourself...
As I did...
From weak to strong,
You just hung on...
And now you have become your own...
We won

Alone

Leave me alone now; it doesn't matter...anyhow...
I need some time, just by myself...
A quiet time of deep reflection...
To heal these wounds of life's rejections
Please leave me alone, for I need to be...
My life's in a whirlwind now; it can not see...
For it has become just as the day is without the sun
I feel alone, inside myself...
The door is closed; I want no help
In time, I'll heal; it shouldn't be long...
In time, I feel...
I'll sing my song
I've made mistakes for sure I know
But...
It doesn't matter... anyhow...
Life does go on; please understand
I withdraw my hand, my heart; they need new start,
A new beginning, a time away
They all are spinning...
Around and around, going nowhere...
When I did search, emptiness was found there
Trapped alone, inside myself
Just leave me alone now...
There is no one else
Just stay away; it is not wrong
Though some might say
This life of mine is void of song now...
My price I pay

Delusion

Delusion…
Silent fantasy
A life that is meant for me
Mirage, painted with reality…
One that brings hurt to me
Delusion…
I'm caught in its net; this trap that's been set
Will never let go…
Drawn in its downward spiral…
Truth has met with rival…
Strong, both will fight:
Who is wrong?
Who is right?
Delusion…
You have lied to me!
I can not see clearly at all…
I know I'll fall
Delusion…
I fight you!
Each night you
Grip hold, I can not breathe…
No one can help
It paralyzes me…
I can't move away
It won't let me go…
My soul melts within…
All I have felt within…
Was mirage

Fall's Wonder

Fall's wonder…
Summer's over…
Winter whispers…
Color splashes bright,
Enhancing our appetite
Feed upon its open store, for no more will its bounty be…
You see…
Love and beauty display fall's color
We look and wonder
As creation displays its excellent array
From its bounty we take, its banquet spread open to all…
Draw from its generosity…
Earth's harvest, life's bequest
Before those winter days,
When life says…
Summer is over,
Winter whispers all life must sleep
And you must keep until…
Spring's birth brings new again…
Then…
We start life again

Free Bird

Free bird
Fly high!
Way up in the autumn sky...
Fly above us, down below...
To us all, your life does show:
No hindrance...
As hindrance be
No distance too far
For you or me...
No dream
That you can't dare...
No fear...
Trust holds you in the air...
No journey
One may molest...
No harm...
God is there to protect
No boundary...
The world is yours
Behold your value...
Above the finest gold
Your message,
Infinite and free...
Live life
With grace and dignity

Along the Way

Along the way, sometimes it seems…
When life grows dark,
No sight of dreams…
When whirlwind blows and clouds the light…
Surpassing desires, hope gives no fight…
When hatred heals the scab on heart…
When bitterness darkens, sours life now tart…
Along the way…
Some day will be
A different way for you and me…
When new growth begins, inside, somewhere…
A deep soul's birth grows new…it's there…
Doubt fades away, hastens hope anew…
Fatalistic thoughts erased,
Now life's a hue

Vision

One small part of all the others...
One world vision with many colors
Equality sees with equal eyes...
Fairness hides no lying lies...
Justice has its open doors,
Giving entrance
To rich and poor...
Future holds eternity in its grip...
Gives to us from cup to drink...
Taste its wonder; you will see...
Peace in plenty, safety free

As the Rose Opens

As the rose opens, hope blossoms
Beauty reveals its secret concealed within tender bud held tight...
From all our sight until...
Silent word is spoken
This mystery wide opens,
So we may see a piece of creativity...
Express itself with dignity
As the rose opens, displaying bright color...
Patterns on its petals, luster
Dew brings its kiss,
Our eyes become enhanced...
Perhaps entranced by beauty's miracle
For...
As the rose opens...
Hope begins

Consider

All our days are numbered,
All our wrongs remembered…
Though we seek to live unhindered,
Responsibility does call…
Showing no favor to any at all
Dignity must respect
To each cause
There is effect…
The fact is universal
Life sets the stage…
There is no rehearsal
To all around, mankind, creation…
Every earthly relation…
Cause pays answer…
Effect responds most naturally
Think, what may seem right to you and me…
Might just bother someone else,
How we behave to one another…
Directly effects humankind…
Could bring disaster,
Whatever mars, destroying life…
You'll pay the price
Suffering shows no partiality…
Cost may be great…
Help may come…
Too late…
Consider these words,
Just weigh them on life's scales,
Imbalance throws one side down…
The other
Suspends without proper ground…
Both hurt one another and all because…
Actions were not considered…
Truth always has rebound
All our days are numbered…
All our wrongs remembered…
They all play out regardless if we agree…
One day, I know…

You'll see

Impulses

Never act on impulse…
Or else…
You will regret what you never meant to be…
Never act on impulse…
Or else…
You'll regret what you did say…
And pay… a bitter price
Think twice…
Maybe what you did intend
Did bend
Now, anger, hopefully mended…
Calmed by forgiveness,
Seasoned with embrace…
Please, make haste; don't linger…
Consider…
For those who are weighed down by regrets,
Some never to forget…
Will live endlessly, forever…
Lives that were severed, shattered by impulse
No thought as to consequence…
Sets the stage hence…
To bitterness

I'm Not Me

I'm not me...
I'm not at all who I want to be...
I can't see...
Who I am
Is mystery...
Sometimes numb with fear...
No one near...
No one listens at all...
I'm small...
Insignificant...
I can't be
Who I want to see...
All alone...
Everyone on the other side
I hide, behind my wall
Behind all those who are tall
Away, beside in no one's land...
No one left
Will take my hand
I guess, I must confess...
I need some time to heal...
So that I may feel
Alive again, my friend
No, I'm not me...
I'm not at all what I want to be
I'm so gripped by fear within,
Can't move within,
Thoughts paralyze
Horrors I surmise...
All those could-have-beens
That could be when...
I believe lies spoken to myself...
Won't someone help?
Inside me melts...
Fear eats away...
My life each day...
No, I can't control these fears, you see...
I'm not me

Hold On

Be encouraged; focus on your dreams
Hold on; just hold on…
One day, they will happen
Have you fallen?
Have you fallen?
Don't cry…
Why?
These things happen
They just happen…
Don't worry…
You'll get by
For in this world are people given special wisdom and strength
They will help you…
Yes, they will help you…
Hold on
You'll win at length
Are you afraid?
Yes, fear still does live within us all
Sometimes, it can choke you…
Its grip is tight
Don't let it hold you…
You have to fight with might from within you
Just fight it!
Just fight it!
It's not stronger than you or I…
Regain new strength
For one day, you will see…
That you have won life's battle
And you will smile within yourself
For people notice these victories, hard to hide
With new wings,
You'll fly

What's in My Heart?

What's in my heart for me today?
What's in my heart?
No words can say…
Emotions,
Devotions, lay deeply connected
All affected by time and others around
Some confound
Astound…
As perceptions rebound
All sound together only to find…
What's in my heart
May alarm, harm, even if forgiven
These thoughts forbidden, foreboding…
Withholding love until…
What's in my heart
Shows itself ill…
Truly, life does sometimes buffet
Though you try to stop it
For a while, but still…
Life does bend us; it lends us
Friends, befriend us
We pretend not to be ourselves…
At times what we feel
Is not allowed
Life is under the clouds…
Nothing shows itself real
Opportunity controls us; it tries to mold us
Emotions that have…
Hold us
Seems like no one to trust
Do what we must
Our heart withers inside
We try to hide what we feel
Life lied
Even loved ones go away…
What's in my heart may have to say…
All that's been stored now,
Has to pour out and over…

No more cover
Secrets will share
My heart will repair
All it has broken...
With its deep token of love, it will mend us
Though it did send us far, far away...
All will be revealed
As fruit that's been peeled
Its pulp full of sweetness, you see...
Life didn't defeat us at last
We may caress...
With deep devotion and shared tenderness
Now...
All that's been denied
Though my heart did try...
Tears that never dried...
Are all wiped away...
Now I'll say...
What's in my heart, the sadness, the sorrow...
Just waiting for all those tomorrows...
All those emotions still painful, do control each day
At times with hatred and dismay
For...
What's in my heart must lie still...
Though circumstances go against will...
All grows darker, perhaps...
Life takes a different course...
Amidst regret and remorse...
Hope grows deeper still...
Until...
Idea becomes a possibility
Making real to me
Giving a chance to me
Will my life yet be?
For all that is in my heart must have its expression
Or else life is but a painful lesson...
Not desiring to be lived, instead...
Death will be the sweeter still,
For...
All that has been denied will lie
Eternity is bliss...

Secret

I've been patiently waiting, for my secret to share...
It's been a long time held within...
But surely, it is there...
Will you patiently listen until my secret unfolds?
Told with much agony and pain
It is too much for my soul to contain...
No longer can it be held within me...
It has been as a weight so heavy
It bends me
I must place it down now...
My heart has strained too long now,
Not wanting to hurt you...
But in all fairness with love, I must tell you...
So plainly...please, just listen...
Just give me your ear
But understand with your heart
I must now share with you...
For we have too long been torn apart
A barrier was formed that must now come down
My secret,
Revealed by truth,
Because I love you...
Freedom must be found

I Am Broken

I am broken...
I am broken...
What do people say?
Pieces of my heart lie...
They lie broken,
They lie broken...
Dreams have been swept away...
Does no one care?
I tried...
I tried...
Always to be there...
I tried to help people...
Tried to listen
Giving...of myself...
Always giving...
To people taking...
Always taking...
All that I am
All that I would have been...
I am broken...
I am broken...
Don't the pieces fit together anymore?
I tried so often...
To fit them back together
Then, no more...
No more could I hold love...
And emotion...
Does reality control our destiny?
Our future?
It's no use now...
For I've been robbed of dignity
You see...
All of its beauty, its patience, its sanity
Are gone from me...
Don't you see?
Inside of me, only emptiness...
And loneliness,
I must confess...

I'm useless
For my gift I possessed,
One that had purpose, value…
Has no hue
There is nothing left for me to do…
So I say to you…I am broken…

Lie

My hands are tied
Your promise lied...
Truth seemed so real
My heart did feel
A love unbound...
For you was found, most freely given...
But leaven leavened...
To you was fed,
Now love lies dead
Now taken back,
Our future bleak
No more to give...
Now life, I dread...
Our well has gone dry...
From spring's source stopped
Now ache holds heart...
Memory desires no part...
Nothingness,
It looms...
Half of me is gone...
This lie
I lived so long...

Esteem

Hold your head high...
But your eyes are not haughty...
Hold your head high
One day someone you will be
With quiet resolve and determination
Resolve to work hard without hesitation...
Know your dreams
Give ear to your inner voice
Carefully prepare from life's choice
Come now what may...
Ignore whatever it is
"They" say...
Hold your head high
Life's a challenge
Whatever it is you do
Sometimes we fall
As many others will too...
What ever error or vice
Try again; heed my advice...
Hold your head high

Journey

How far a distance?
How near a star?
How great a journey?
A small part of life we are...
How high a mountain?
How deep the sea?
What part of this world was I destined to be?
How deep the valley?
How many times does a river bend?
How many days are portioned out for me
until this journey ends?
Is there anyone who understands reasons why
we can?
I think over these questions...
For weighty they are
Some in this life wander aimless...
Some go very far...
Some do mostly nothing...
For they are the center of themselves
Shallowness...all callousness...their journey isn't far...
Some go to many places, see the world, respect different faces
Contributing with what they learn in life
Helping others to cope, to stand, to fight...
Gaining victories, many types there are...
Soothing misery, so many varieties...
Some scoff at all of these...mocking what they do,
Yet, their journeys end
When justice deems it through
The truth about our ways you see...
Begins with what we are to be
How our actions go about two ways...
One leads to fulfillment, the other only misbehaves
What we do with our lives really does matter
Either makes things grow,
Or simply scatters...
One path leads to another, strengthens brother to brother, sister
to sister...
But the other path...destiny blocks its way

For confusion and misdirection
Don't have much to say
Simplistic in its analogy
Truthful as is reality
Weigh them out between the two…
Which one seems right for you?

Line and Formation

Line and formation,
Break away two...
Earth and creation
Have their reason...
To do...
Geese fly in formation...
Order is planned
Searching for destination...
Security commands
Each season brings change...
Time runs the clock
Life has its reasons
No one can stop
Unity
Position...
Safe haven glistens...
Instruction
Direction
Point to their goal...
In spite of the weather...
Disaster...
Mal-factor...
Purpose brings together,
Trust secures the call
Where are all going?
They seem to be...
Just following
Line and formation
Each and every destination
Instinct beyond you...
Safe habitation dwells true

For All I Know

For all I know…
Love has no limit
For all I know…
Love's deep fathoms never inhibit…
Trust builds its foundation
Relationship holds its coronation
Faithfulness treasures its vow
Fidelity displays her golden glow
For all I know…
Together we will be
Here in this life,
Until we see
Eternity…
Its ocean shore gathering glimpses
Of what lies in store…
Love in its existence
Will always be…
Self and worth dine together…
Value esteem,
Come quickly, truth calls to you now…
For all I know…
As life goes on…
Somehow

Cloudy Days

On those cloudy days, when mood sets in...
Sun's rays are gone,
All is dark and dim
Those cloudy days...
When outlook is overshadowed,
Perspective changes
From deep to shallow...
How I hate those days;
So strange they seem...
When clouds move in,
Now on their own
Leaving us here below,
Just wondering why...
Beyond ourselves...
Dark days
They come...
No one's exempt
They shadow everyone...
There is nothing we may do
But wait...
With patience and hope...
Let heart not hate
For the sun will shine...
It does come again
Its rays cascade
While broken hearts mend
Each cloudy time will fade away...
Love heals all
Without price to pay...
As the sun befriends,
Giving strength to hang on...
Clouds are gone...

Through the Eyes of a Child

Through the eyes of a child, all the world is a wonder
In them is innocence, tenderness, need
A medley of song, and laughter…
Surely we must love them,
Protect and defend them…
A child…
So consuming
Energy flowing, they are amply supplied!
Do we try to deny it?
For sometimes we mar them,
Sometimes by hatred, violence…even stardom
Though they may cry, each in their own way,
"I have not yet lived; I have something to say…
I still am so tender; I'm not ready for life
And all it does render…
Please hold me; keep me safe, until…
Let me grow useful, let me develop
Don't let the world kill…
Let me be unhindered, unmutilated, uninfluenced until…
My future unfolds,
My destiny made real
I will share; I will give, all my abilities given…
I don't want to become
A victim
I don't want to be used
I'm not anyone's fool
My future, opportunity dictates; prosperity calls."
But… poverty to some threatens;
Alcohol and drugs mar and kill…
Broken homes make children wander
Innocent lives are spilled
Please…won't you just help? Don't let them suffer
Spare them…you see, they are not the world's buffer…
All this hatred, all this pitiful strife,
Don't deny them a father, a mother,
We need to live together…
Dignity must clothe them; grace must adorn their heads
Truth must be taught to them

Living honestly, without dread
Character must develop; children really must live,
Don't you all see?
In order for children to be…
Whatever gifts they possess won't happen,
Unless
The world, parents, adults alike…
All must unite…
Children need to be shown not what's wrong,
But what's right…
Children have to learn:
One must love, not fight..
As complex as this may seem,
All could have beens
Could be
Let them grow
Gifted and free…
For to a child,
All the world is a wonder
Allow it to be
All the world is a wonder
For children…
So please…

Flip Side

What ever happened to you?
I thought, I really thought
I knew…
Everything about you
Seemed so good…
Now…it seems as if another side of you
Stood…
Different, distant, dark at times…
Must be your flip side,
The dark side…
The half that lay hidden
Forbidden for us all to see…
Even me…
Must be your flip side…
The other half I'd never seen before,
Little did I know what lay in store,
For me…
Please,
I want your other part,
The side with heart…
The soft side
Make me alive again
Be my friend…
Please show me the side I know…
The one that makes me glow
With happiness and romance
Enhance me
With your flip side,
The right side; then…
Hand in hand,
We stand united,
Not divided…
You see, I need your flip side…
Change over again
Hearts mend…
Flip side…

Which do I now see?
Is it the one I want it to be?
Give me your flip side,
The right side; the other…hide
My sweet, then…
Let's start over again

Art Through an Open Door

Art through an open door
Walk through it, you will see
Never ending comfort, releasing, free...
Hours with no expectation,
No worry, no one to harass...
Quietly expressing...
Deep from within,
Anxiety will pass
Away through an open door
Come quickly...
Abide...
Refuge will offer strong protection,
Healing constant
As the noon day tide

Touché

Touché…
We touch…
The challenge has begun…
Touché…
We duel…
Hatred set apart
Two hearts that were one
Love's braided cord severed,
A devil's sword hovers between…
Touché…
We touch…
The fight is on...
Our swords are drawn…
The masks are worn; this dare goes on…
With challenging looks…
Both spite and hooks,
Glances given as thrusting javelin…
Voices spoken…
Iced with hate…
No deeds of kindness, no moments of laughter,
No thoughts of one another…instead…
Touché
We touch…
We challenge each other,
For difference overtakes…
Now, opinions dominate…
No respect towards one another of late…
This game, our duel, began when thoughtlessness bred,
Unkind demand,
Hope's store worn out
Unforgiveness pressed heavy,
Floods of disagreement
Overpowered each one's levy
Hearts that once united were
Now hold drawn swords
Vows forgotten, promises made…
Never begotten…
As decay makes rotten…

Love's storehouse drained
While masks of hardness were put on
Each face becoming our protection,
Each defense holding no affection…
Disclosed feelings concealing all
But hardness…
No caress…now only emptiness…
This duel of ours!…
Why is it your goal to make me cower?
Why do you make me feel that I'm lower?
Then…
A step you take back, by two…
As I advance towards you…
And now…
At times I fear…
You see!
Touché
We touch…
You look at me…
Touché
You scoff at me!
Then…
I dare you with my words!…
Touché
We touch…
With both our swords!
And yet…if we both would just reflect…
There was a time
When we found joy in one another…
Closer than brothers we both were…
And now…
We look like fools!
Place down your sword
This challenge must end!
Bend pride,
Let love open both hearts wide…
Remember those years we shared together?
Even thru tears and sacrifices?
When patience weathered each others vices?
When emotions understood,
As no one else would…

When weakness invoked gentle caress?
Waiting arms protected from life's harm...
Our swords weren't drawn...
Against each other...
They fought together!
Against life's friction,
This duel's intensity wears the best of us down...
Touché
Renounce!
I say...I do!
These words, my vow... I gave to you!...
Though long ago...
Someone I knew
Stood beside me,
Taking my hand
Please, no more duel...
It's gone far beyond cruel,
So foolish
I place down my sword...
I give you my word!
No more *touché* my love...unless...
Touché, my love...
To kiss

Demands

Each day brings life's happenings…
Ups and downs,
Tossing emotions around…
Direction pulls
Each its own way…
Weight and pressure
Have equal say
Responsibility desires to accomplish all
While the rug gets pulled out from under,
Causing a fall…
Whatever the cost, whatever the wish is,
Demands are hard
One sees each need…
Conflicts arise
Want to bend the rules…for necessity
Necessitates…
Then dislike comes in,
Doing what it hates…
Vow battles all,
But somehow gets through…
Though vision may blur…
(It can happen to you!)
Direction sees steadfast…as it leads
Until deliverance ends,
Brings one where they hope to be…
Now you see what you want to see,
Just keep your eye single
Focus on your goal,
Though your journey be slow,
Let values not mingle…
Though your choices be narrow
And the ground you stand fallow
Whatever it is you do…
Demands
Will always happen,
Coming even
From you…

All I Ever Wanted Was You

All I ever wanted
Was you…
To feel about me
The way I feel about you…
To see inside…
To never hide…
All I ever wanted…
Was you
Right from the start
My heart was drawn
Inside I felt,
It was you I'd charmed
You never let harm come my way…
Close beside me,
You always stayed…
You made my life so right,
You see…
No one else but you
Will be
Mine, until death comes our way
Until that day
We are but one
No other to glance…
None other to romance…
Our lives enhance
Each other in so many ways…
For all our days…
Inside me says…
All I ever wanted was you

Play

Let's play today
The sun is shining…
Our lives are young
There is nothing we are hiding
For life is fun…
No cares have we
Other than wanting
To be loved,
To be free…
Hand in hand, we will play
Painting pictures within our minds
Happily, so merrily…
Serious or dramatic…
We enter in
Within the door of our imagination
But we are told
By grown ups alike…
That fun will flee
As life will be
So full of surprises
And it will change
Sometimes with pain
It will all be different…
So play this day…
It is okay,
The sun is shining…
But know for sure…
My friend,
Its true
That it will change,
For me…and
For you…

Michelangelo

Michelangelo...
Your name does glow
As angelic forces in the heavenly skies
Why won't mankind
Look to you again
As friend?
A message you did bring
Your gifts of love
Made our hearts sing
Of majestic beauty your sculptures were
Tenderness in marble did express
The skill you possessed
Meant to be...
A miracle yes...
Overlooked you are, my friend
Forgotten...put away
How can it be?
Your life the world did see
So often...but
Focus has changed
Technology numbs our minds
Takes imagination away
Empties conscience of thought
In its web we are caught
Rekindle fascination
To Michaelangelo's creations
The pinnacle of masterpiece...
The Sistine...
Such silent force!
Can't you see it?
It goes beyond logic...
Expressed from within...
As creativity has always been
Until it is seen,
Just look again...

Children's Song

I hear the sound of many voices,
Of children…
They are playing,
Laughing together…
Each one's different,
Some quite higher or lower…
Louder…softer…
Still, they are all but one…
Coming together
Just to have fun…
Unity,
Friendship
Diverse…yet coming together to play,
To sing…
The voices to blend
Harmony in unity…
A priceless jewel!
Life's reward from pleasure
Because all are true to mankind
Why don't we see it?
Peace; don't conceal it…
All can play together
A harmonious tune
Sweet to the inner ear,
With nothing to fear
Only enjoying each other's company…
In harmony…
All are one
Just listen to
the children's song

Remember Me

Dedicated to Tom Poore – who died of cancer on March 1, 2000
To his wife, Patti, and children: David, Danny, and Krista
Remember me,
Though eyes can't see
Person to person...
Life it seems, always so uncertain, constantly changing present
reality...
As it did both to you and me...
Remember me...
Thoughts from afar bring nearness closer...
Time and place can't take all away...
For...
Memories stay
Draw from recollection life's past collection...
Until...
Broken hearts mend
Then...
Though one may be separated
Though reality is hurtful,
And hated...
Remember me...
Love covers all
Your guardian will be...
Remember me...
Though the flower is gone...
Seeds remain
Even those planted through tears and pain
Love lingers...
It's legacy is left for you
Given to all those whom
Sadness left behind
Love's not blind,
It has eyes that see all need...
Reaching down to you,
Upholding you...
Love never walks away...
For now I'll say...
Remember me...

Each moment shared together
Will be there
With you together
Etched forever in time
Yes, memory holds them
As life unfolds them
Heat treasures them forever...
When you remember me
With new eyes you'll see...
Love goes on

Hindrances and Obstacles

Hindrances and obstacles like tentacles surround us...
Confound us...
They hound us...
Making us cease to be...
You see hindrances and obstacles like burrs;
They stick to us
Confronting us, frustrating us, every day
In many forms they come
And some...
Even pretend to love
But...
They hate and abuse us
In whatever form they may
From day to day,
Even years of hell...
Like bars upon a prison cell...
Hindrances and obstacles try to overtake us,
Control us
So that we never live
And then...
One day perhaps
You will see...
That hindrances and obstacles
As viruses
Overtaken by good cells
Are consumed —
Found no more
Enjoy life's store
Without them, my friend...
Grow now as the green, green grass
At last...
You may live life without the weeds
Now there is no need
For those that took
Life's nourishment...
Encouragement is offered to you now...
For somehow...
Hindrances and obstacles lie broken

They have all been shattered
Now, all that mattered
You are free
To be

Science

Dedicated to Mr. Backus

Science
Is the alliance
Of creatures in creation...
Each has its proper station
In a world we see, taste and feel...
Science is real,
Living active among us
Kingdom, phylum, and order...
There can be no disorder...
Or else extinction will be...
Family, genus, and species...
Teachers will always teach these...
There is no monotony here...
Science has tremendous appeal
For the gift of life is amazing
Even Galileo spent much of his time...
Gazing
Leonardo and Michelangelo
Reverenced these many miracles
For what began as mystery.
Revealed itself through science, you see...
Whatever subject or topic...
Of the universe
Or microscopic...
All play an important role
In the circle of life
With survival is its goal
Science upholds all these valuable things...
Learn of them
To mankind, great benefit will bring...

Beyond Now

Go beyond now…
The present isn't all you see
For…
Beyond now,
There is so much more to life
For you to be…
Go deeper…
Dig your roots in the soil…
That is thicker
And richer…
You will find before the flower grows,
The blossom takes its time
Life's nourishment draws beauty from an unseen source
Follow this true course,
Turn eyes away from all that glistens…
Listen…
Real wisdom calls out to all
It shall keep you from life's final fall…
Beyond even now…
Eternity draws each one closer
Weakness is strengthened
When will lies broken
Love displays its precious token
Giving its gift with words unspoken
Beyond now, one day you'll see…
A different person
A jewel
Meant from eternity
To be

Hideaway

There is a place where you may go...
And hide away
From world and care
To be set free...
And...
Hide away
Inside of conscience, heart and thought...
Precious freedom to exist
Away from fear and pressures
You may dwell...
And...
Hide away
This place,
This precious hide away,
Is within us all, if I may say
All are different,
Special to each of us
Tailored, they fit together just well
Experience peace,
Be set free...
To just be...
Without all the rest
Go; hide away...
Just meditate
Escape the world,
And life's cruel taste...
Be free...
Yes, both you and me...
Just imagine...
Liberty...
In its truest sense,
It is our natural self-defense
Defies walls built all around
It goes beyond even limitation...
Our minds,
What powerful creations!
Possess this miracle,
And hide away...

Reality won't find you
For the two
Won't play

Our Love

Love that is denied
Is hard to hide
Leaving traces and shadow
Of melancholy,
So lonely…
If only…
Oh, if only…
I did not have to deny…
Why?
Why?
Can't our love show?
For surely it did grow…
It did blossom as a beautiful tree
It did become…
Two as one…
But complications did hinder
As does life often so…
Oh no…
Oh no…
If only circumstances were different
But they sometimes control us
Why do they hold us from each other?
It is but painful to remember
The times we shared together
Are they all to be forgotten?
No…
Always treasured they will be
This strange and twisted life did lie to us,
To both of us
Our hearts were open to the world,
And especially to each other
I do not understand
For hand and hand we walked together,
United, understanding one another
Without words…
Just understood
So much alike,
But kept apart…

Oh how?
Oh how?
I dread the day
For now we pay a painful price
Not once, but twice cut short…
No more together
Surely it does hurt so…
For…
Love that is denied
Is hard to hide
The days of dread,
In years ahead
I can't deny
I can't deny

On the Edge

On the edge...
Yes, I am living on the edge...
Caught from both sides
No where to hide...
Peace of mind...
It escapes me...
Pressures constantly increasing,
Releasing
Emotions of despair...
I live in constant fear...
Depressions go deeper
Volition...
It seeps through...
Silent tears...
No one cares
Anxiety engulfs me...
Dark thoughts,
They assault me...
I cannot see
Decision
Escapes me
Fear takes over now
It is stronger than I
Why?
Why must life be this way?
All that I am
Sways
Change has overtaken
Identity...
I'm not me
Nothing is clear
Inside me...
Does not hear...
No one near to encourage...
For I
Am living on the edge
My life
Remains as existence

On sharp precipice
I look down to see death below…
Its mouth is open wide…
Its bite
Holds eternity for me
Can't you see?
Indecision…
Taunts me
These voices within…
They haunt me…
Failure comes to take me away…
Until…
Hope sparks will
Fight begins within
Though my life lies grim…
Hope's voice is soft and small
What makes it stronger still?
I know…
Love will
Just let it be
To me it whispers encouragement now
Why did it come so late?
It was almost overtaken
By hate
Sometimes I guess…
Love's hesitation
Lets time think over our lives
Again…
And then...
Today…
One must listen
Truth's clear voice
Glistens
It calls us from darkness somehow…
Drawing us closer now…
Rationale takes over,
Along with hearts guidance,
Our lives grow enhanced
We walk away from our precipice…
For…
Love's safe haven rescues us from all our fears

Until...
No more tear are cried
Now, no need to hide from life again...
We're safe, my friend

Loneliness

Loneliness often, deep inside
Always there, though it tries to hide
For where you go,
It does follow
Thru crowded streets…
Rooms full of people,
Family, friends…
It still does haunt you,
Holding tightly with its grip
Grabbing your heart…
Those strings do rip
We cannot shake it…
Music, friendship,
Entertainment, pleasure…
It still comes upon you…
Until an ache is formed within the heart
Why?
Is something in life still missing?
A part of you, keeps still insisting
That something inside is gone…
It's just not there though it is crucial
To survival
Surely there are countless reasons why…
Though attempt may try and try…
As an illness can transform you,
Changing a vibrant life…
To weakness often,
This unseen illness
Loneliness…
Leads to depression
Day by day your will
Does lessen
Until despair gives its final blow
Inside your heart…
There is no more glow
Pill nor bottle, doctor, friend…
Nothing mends the tear inside
The loneliness and the fear…

Though people listen...they do not hear...
The tears cried silently inside
Difficult for you to really explain
Deep inside your soul's own pain
Relentless,
Loneliness...Will be

Nicknames
Dedicated to my daughter, Brittany

Sometimes a name
Becomes a game…
It can happen as it does,
Often
To you or to me
Sometimes funny,
Sometimes curt…
Often times though,
Nicknames hurt!
Do we need them?
Some people think so
Others would rather let them go…
But when all is said…
(From within the head…)
You may just dread
What they will call you
But say no more…
Can one ignore
The ignorance and disrespect?
A nickname can yet be given
Out of love,
Just sent from heaven…
(But rarely so…)
Usually they just distort
A name to one's own hurt!
So think before you speak;
A nickname can really bother…
A sister, brother,
a father, or mother…
Even relative or friend…
There is no end…
You can apply them
To anyone…just to poke fun
So be careful before you name a "nick"
For one day, a nickname on you might stick!
A nickname…

A short cut...a disrespect...a jest?
Remember, please,
Though they may form with ease...
A nickname is oftentimes
A tease!
So please don't use them; think before you speak...
To call a name can make someone inside feel weak...
...And small, not tall at all!
They will dread what you just said...
Learn to respect your neighbor,
Father, brother, mother...
It is what's right to do
More peace will come
Unity becomes the sum
Friendships will blossom
Even love, often...
The world, our home does need this so...
Take all those nicknames...
And just let them go...

Andrea

Andrea…
Though blindness touched your eyes,
Life was never hidden from you…
Andrea…
A marvel to all you are,
You have traveled far in life, in melody…
How beautiful you are to me…
To be so unhindered,
Trusting others for sight…
Though arms reach out to you,
Yours reach out to speak
Hidden truths of courage and strength
To what unlimited lengths you go in life each day
With hope fueling your strength from within
It makes us grin…
When we see our own limitations
No humiliation…
We break out and away from what holds us down
Just push it away, Andrea…
Empowered…
In life…
Savor its wonder…
Experience unlimited doors to open,
Free you are from judging others
Just living, caring, giving…
Andrea…
Continue on in life's song
Sing on…

High on a Hill

High on a hill...
Thoughts are lofty
Oh! How softly voices speak,
Silently scoffing...
For...
High on a hill
You don't know until
People down below look above; they wonder...
Such grandeur, how can it be?
From the same human race we come...
What's happened?
Why do you have so much more than all the rest?
Why does life give only you its best?
What have you taken?
What have you forsaken?
You've tipped the scales on your behalf,
Holding others down,
While your hands greedy, grasp
I hesitate...
I wonder...
Why has fate put the rest of us under?
Toil and sweat
As rain and thunder
Mark our low land
We've all put in with heart and hand...
Intelligence is given to all of mankind
To everyone gifts are given, you'll find...
But...
Why are all those high on a hill
Becoming richer?
Better?
Greater?
Until...
Whim becomes the sum of them
Their noses point upward;
Their eyes become lofty...
Everything they do
Is costly...

Vanity speaks, loud and clear
To them, possessions outnumber need
Now it seems, noticing with anger
That both you and me
Suffer defeat
In conclusion,
Mixed with sadness and perplexity,
Life it seems…
A mess to me…
Why live at all?
Our lives are painful…
While they rest above
Peering down…disdainful…
Discomfort, far from them, surrounded by extravagance,
Their lives continually enhanced with luxury and ease…
While with haughty looks they tease…
Taunting…
Continually flaunting,
Comparing what they possess…
While we live in toil and constant distress
But…
I hold a secret,
Something more precious to inherit…
For all those high on a hill…
There is judgment still…
Your strong tower
Won't last forever
What prosperity now…
Fate will sever
Your material gain
Will bring you pain
It will bring birth to stubble…
On yourselves, you will bring your own trouble
You will get what you deserve
Though now you serve yourself with pleasure
You are not above
Fair measure
Arrogance…
All your polish
Will be demolished
One day, you will be low…

Even though visions of yourselves were tall...
Not realizing...
Not sympathizing...
Thinking yourselves high on a hill
Pride and strong will...
Humbles
As it crumbles
Life will bring you down like all the rest...
Look at yourselves in life's mirror...
All cherished splendor is defiled
All the while you thought yourselves richer...
Now those beneath you
Smile as they see you face to face...
Level
With spot and wrinkle,
We all have the same likeness...
All this human race shares the same face (*dignity*)
Try as we might, this sight,
High on a hill...
Must be no more

War's Sorrow

Dedicated to all those involved in the terrible calamity of WWII
Written for my son, Marc

A cancer grows when hate begins...
Human conflict leads to death within
"Nation against nation, rumors of war..."
Anxiety speaks, destruction flares
All lead to human misery
Betrayal, defiance, national alliance
Create a force so great
All powered by hate...
The leaders...
The killers
Lead an unmerciful spree
Of death and torture
To Jews and gypsies...
Anyone who stood against their will
They'd kill...
They'd kill...
Hitler, Stalin, and Mussolini
Created an alliance...
The terrible three...
All went well until betrayal brought down
An empire of evil, as bombs did pound...
Great lands destroyed, monuments crumbled...
Soldiers in tents, as life was humbled...
Germany, Italy stood alone
Until Japan did come along...
An error so great
As brought by fate
Destroyed a safe Harbor...
A Pearl of America's labor...
A surprise attack...
A horrible toll...
Struck America, bringing our country low...
Strike against strike
A new power takes birth
An eagle flies, for life is worth

Soldiers are sent to right a wrong
Patriotism sings its national song...
World War II, a just cause stands
Our lands regained while hand in hand...
Though life is lost and tears are shed
A ray of hope shines while troops are led
And as turmoil proceeds,
Unity gains strength while victory leads...

Always and Forever

Always and forever
You and I will be…
Always and forever
Forming a bond so strong
Hanging on so long…
Neither time nor separation
Gave way to doubt…
No hesitation…
We both realize before our very eyes
Nothing else but you will be…
Always and forever
Don't listen to what people say
Careless they are
Come what may…
They don't know
What we show is deep, inside
Come my love,
With me abide…
They can't love…
They don't know how…
Misunderstood we will be…
For our love was destiny
What matters they will never see
Try to explain…
Futility…
You and I, we both need to be…
Always and forever…
Time waste no more…
Always and forever…

Life Story

I'm aging, old...
My story is told...
Now I wait...
My life is late; thoughts flee within...
Days grow grim...
I feel as if an open grave calls...
Retroflection taunts,
Bringing deep regret...
All those years...
Love beckoned, yet...
Truth did deny
As I, turning with my back...
I lied...
Too late now...
Too little of me was given...
Life's endless sorrow
Will be my tomorrow...
But it was my choice
I denied life's inner voice
Now with deep regret,
I must pay my debt...
Eternity becomes a grave's hollow
I know many will follow...
I leave an empty legacy
All that dies...
Is me...

I Can

I am
I can…
I'll be…
You'll see…
In me, a different person…
I'm certain…
My eyes will shine
And I will dine
On worth,
Within…
Around…
Confound…
Those who just took
From me with hook
(*in soul*)
I'm free…
To be…
Myself…
With help
Of grace
And strength…
I'll win at length…
And be…
And be…
Just me…

Housewife

I'm loosing heart;
I can not start my day…
It seems so futile…
To dwell inside…
I cannot hide my sadness…
I feel so little…
How long to go?
Such depths, so deep…
I feel…
And still, I seek an answer…
What is my life?
Am I just a wife?
A maid in kitchen?…
With knife and fork…to cook…to clean…
Not to demean such call…
I want much more…
To give, to live,
To reach all my potential…
I do hope so…
That I may go…
Much further…
Without recourse…
With no remorse…
My voice, my choice, my call…
Today I'll start
With hope in heart
A new path…
A new journey to begin
To give, to live, I'm on my way…
In part, to start with mind
And heart
My voice, my choice, my call…
…and be
…and be
Just me

Young Child

Young child
Tender and mild,
I will love you…
I will hold you…
So dear to my heart you are…
Your tiny form
I will tenderly adorn
You are most free
A part of me…
Oh, can it be,
Such a gift to treasure?
Love…
Without measure, your bounty be…
Please come to me
I will hold you…
I will embrace you…
Forever in my heart…
One day, I know we'll part…
And you will start a new life's course…
Yet my love will tenderly endorse…
Mixed with remorse…
I'll let you go…
I'll let you go…
Young child,
Tender, mild…
It will hurt,
I know…
I know…

Depression

Depression…
Melancholy obsession,
Death within the soul…
A wounded heart,
No joys to impart…
Seeds unplanted,
Un-watered, un-sprouted…
Camouflaged by life
Having to go on…
Nothing within…
A prisoner of gloom…
No room
For living as others do…
Separated…
Nothing but hatred
Only loneliness within,
And strife…
Not caring to win,
Life
No sharing of happiness…
Obstacles stand as walls closing in…
Moving in…
On all sides…
I hide
Within myself…
No one can help…
Stares of indifference
Buffet me with hindrance…
No smiles,
Just sadness…
From madness?
No,…
Though the world would say so…
Go deeper I must…
There is no one I may trust…
Help lies beyond…
It's in my mind…
Meditation…

Life will miss this revelation…
To busy to see,
Hearts that are hard
Desire only revelry…
But to you and me…
Depression is an open door…
I see it; walk thru…
You can do it…
Close your eyes to doubt and despair…
I care…

Carousel

Carousel, carousel
Round and round you go...
In happiness and with laughter,
You just go faster and faster...
With music and melody
You make us free...
Why do we love you so?
I don't know...
It seems as if the faces of children and adults alike
Have bliss on them
Though it is just round and around you go...
To the same music over and over
Still they ride on...
And on...
With faces turned up towards the sun
Just holding on...
The surrounding decoration
Holds everyone's fascination
The music controlling what is flowing within each heart
Carousel...
Oh, Carousel...
You are what life was meant to be...
Careless and free...
A temporary heaven?
Faces with bliss on them?
Without hurt, or care?
Surely, I'll pay the fare and ride on...
And on...
Endlessly...
Forever...
It does make us happy
With canopy over our heads
Is its decoration merely for show?
I don't think so...
It keeps us together, protected
It is bliss...
It is free...
Both for you...

And for me
Carousel…
Carousel…
Now I know why
You are loved
So well…

Eternity

Some say it is a matter of opinion...
But I don't think so...
It used to be men were always right
When they had rule...
Total dominion...
Just think about it
Be fair...
Be still...
Meditate...
Why do men hate?
Why do they kill?
It is but life's bitter pill,
So hard to swallow...
We've become so distorted,
Bent as crooked as crooked may go
Listen, as the news reported...
So sordid...
Where will we all go?
Life is more than just to be free
There is more to life than this
What gain?
Revelry to inflict pain?
Let's mend
Turn hatred right about
Bend emotion to have
No distortion
This time, please...
No death...
No disease...
Can we be free from all this?
What would there be to miss?
It's but heaven's kiss
Let it open our lives
It is within you
Go as far as you may go
Rid yourself of arrogance
And pride...
Throw away hatred...

No more to hide…
Eternity may reach out to you
Don't turn your back as others do
Silently, so patiently
Its arms are open
It may one day embrace you…
Make haste, I say to you…
Love is there

You Betrayed Me

You betrayed me...
You betrayed me...
Don't you see what you have done?
You betrayed me...
You betrayed me...
You broke apart
What was one...
It didn't seem to matter
What we shared has now been shattered
You betrayed me...
You betrayed me...
I'm left undone
How could you have violated
A love so carefully created?
So deep, so tender
A man and woman's love
Did render...
Kindness and compassion
Dignity and passion...
A love so pure...
So pure to me...
I was so sure
Forever would be...
Eternity to keep its treasure...
A love so deep,
No one could measure...
Never did I ever imagine...
A disregard of love
Could happen...
You betrayed me...
You betrayed me...
I'm left undone
There is nothing now to trust in...
For a dagger has been thrust in
My heart,
Pierced thru...
So violated
All I feel now is

Humiliated…
Lust has now undone
The cords of love
Evil has won
Now I harbor hatred
Toward myself
You're not attracted…
I can not be
What I thought you saw in me…
Love, has departed…
Emptiness and loneliness… now…
You've become hard hearted….
No direction for me
The rift is thru…
All that's left for me…
I must now do…
You betrayed me…
You betrayed me…
Yes, we're through

Impatience

Impatience…
I'm in haste with my world…
I do worry
All is scurry…
With little time to care…
Impatience…
No common sense….
At times all hindrance and mess!
This race we're in
Has worn patience thin…
Life is so fast paced…
I'm going to be late!
How I hate this whirlwind I'm caught up in…
I'm always behind…
Gotta compete with everyone else…
I'm all nerves and tense…
This all makes no sense…
At all!
What arrogance…
A narrow miss!
He took my turn…
Within me burns…a desire to give back what he deserves…
I swerve…
Now I'm caught up in
Impatience's net
Relaxation melts…
Time has no place at all!
I run and fall…
Competition taunts…
Competing with everyone else
Try to beat the best…
Though the hurdle is high
I can do if I try…
But
Impatience breeds…
"no one else"…
It seems as though…
Influence wins…

80

When greedy greed grins
Bribing all away…
Whatever the cost will pay…
But to me…It says…
Just wait a minute…
This world does have…
Serenity in it…
Just take some time
You'll find
Peace within…
Take a deep breath in…
Impatience
Makes no sense…
Time has its place
There is no race…
Be still…
You don't need that pill!
Relaxing helps…
Helter skelter melts…
Do away with needless care…
You won't run behind…
Or maybe it's time…
This human race…
Does have its place
Do your life correct…
Give and get respect…
Slow down!
Control your own…
Life…
you see…
For…
Impatience hurts
Both you and me

You Never Loved Me

You never loved me...
You never loved me...
Though in pretence you did say...
You never loved me...
You never loved me...
Threads of hatred frayed away...
All of love's potential...
All its ability
To say in many ways and forms
I love you and...
I need you...
Maybe, sometimes
A form of love was there...
Sometimes I thought...
I really thought...
Circumstances showed you cared...
Though in bits and broken pieces...
Sometimes off
Sometimes on...
Thru years of silent sleeping,
I found love meant nothing...
Nothing was really there
Slowly love did wane...
It was painful...
So distressing...
Your heart was hard
There was coldness...no confessing...
There was little or no
Caressing...
Love slowly ebbed away
Now...only
Abandonment and hatred...
Like cancer,
Destroying a love meant to be
Forever...
Nothing like it so precious...
Now only
Callousness...

I know it's hopeless…
For, love lies dormant…
It is sleeping
Each bitter day shows me…
There is only…this answer…*go your way*

On the Inside

On the inside
All beauty is hidden...
To eyes outside,
Forbidden...
For reasons yet unknown
As each one owns
Treasures exist pure within...
To lure within...
All those who have eyes to see...
For...
On the inside...
All is revealed...
Concealed only to the world outside...*for now...*
Beauty hides...
It protects itself, for it values worth
Choosing not to share
Gifts that are there by birth,
Within...
Until the right time calls
Choosing the one on whom the lot falls...
But when...
Judgment condemns...
Friend loses friend...
Vanity mocks,
Pointing fingers at difference
Unaware of what is on the inside...
Robbing mankind...
Keeping for themselves...
Marring creativity's work
Of dignity and worth
Both are pushed away...
So sad to say...
But...
On the inside...
A beautiful city glimmers...
Its existence shared by those who know so well...
Creativity, intelligence
Foundations for what brings life, hence...

Its substance is strong
Knowing right from wrong…
Now vision proceeds ahead
Drawing energy from soul's wellspring…
Bringing treasures for all to see…*for*…
What is *on the inside*…now *will be*…

Deception

Deception...
Father of lies...
A trap has been set
Truth can't deny...
If it holds you,
Your eyes will not see...
Cruelty...
As life was never meant
To be...
Maybe it will hurt you...
Yes, track you down...
Prove to you
What you trusted in...
Can not be found...
Maybe never intended...
Originally...
Deception...
Life's cruel joke...
Happens most naturally
Don't let it hold you...
Control you...
Though it does try...
One day your eyes will open...
Forcing you to say...
"I know what you are!"
"I see through you now!"
Fight deception and lies...
Reach new height of wisdom...
With changed eyes one sees...
Reality happens
One must face deception
Reveal its painful disguise
You'll be stronger, wiser,
Yes, your own master...
Deception eats away at virtue...
All that is true...
Stand against lies...
Your only defense

Is you…
Truth is mighty…
Giving strength to us all…
Start new; with confidence,
Knock down the walls of hindrance
Though deception hurt you…
Rid yourself of weakness
And pride…one must not hide…
Lift your head,
Though your life is changed…
You will not dread
Emotions…
Betrayal…
They weaken and defeat
But we all must meet
Deception…
Silent enemy…
Will always be…

Children of Columbine

Children of Columbine...
Thoughts of you will always be cherished...
Though you did perish
Killed by those with evil intent...
Those that were from hell, sent...
Though they did kill you
And abuse you...
Your lives will always be cherished
Within our minds...
Our hearts reach out...
To your families
Now without...
Your precious presence
Yes, life's sentence touched you
There was nothing
That we could do...
But cry...
Anguish is felt the world over...
A sobering thought...
A moment in time...
When life's candle did flicker...
Diminish...
Put out with pain
Sometimes, life is insane...
It makes no sense at all...
What matters?
Life, in its youth
Marred by those who were uncouth...
Mother's hearts never to soothe
Pain will always be felt
This event left a most terrible welt
Inflicted in chaos and hate
Evil will never abate
Until it is dealt its final blow...
I know so...
Children of Columbine
In God's presence you are...
Complete...

Nothing is marred
Beautiful, now to behold
As your story is told
Eternally now…
How we love you…
Though we never met…
Perhaps, someday we will
Though you swallowed life's bitter pill
You are victors now…
May God caress
Those that you miss…
And gather together
All left behind…
Beloved….
Children of Columbine

Too Little, Too Late

Too little…too late…
This world has corroded…
Too little…too late…
Humankind lies broken…
So much hate…
So much lying…
People dying…
So many crying…
While rich ones denying poor…
For sure,
A downward spiral has begun
All because…
Too little…
Too late…
Hearts are hard
Bent on pride
Self…
Pleasure…
Fun…
Without measure,
Mankind
Is no more treasured
As it once was…
All because…
Too little, too late…
People wanting to kill…
Until…
All is theirs…
With none to share…
Love has gone away
It has departed…
Love hides itself while
Lawlessness runs wild
Bickering, fighting
No lighting of candles
Rich ones leasing
Life giving necessities
Just to increase

Their own ease...
No peace...
For the poor are dying
While rulers are lying...
No one trying to save at all...
People are starving...
As the wealthy are carving...
Legacy
Too little, too late...
Hatred has done its destructive work
In short, hope flickers
As a candle barely burning
Not knowing if its light will shine again
Please listen...
Friend,
Lend a hand; feel with your heart
Someone must start
The world does need to begin again,
What will the world become?
Yes, the world needs transformation
Within each nation...
Human history must forget technology
For a while...
For what worth are treasures
If humankind is gone...
It won't take long...
The world will melt...
Face reality...
Truth speaks
It has given its wake up call
Spread kindness
Feel compassion...
Behold life's painful lesson...
Society needs peace
What will our future hold?
We will all pay if we continue
All will lie broken in the end
All will loose *if we choose...*
Let hatred dissipate...
Vaporize...
Erase all lies...

Build upon trust
We must!
Forget pomp and show…
Hide hypocrisy and aristocracy
Democracy is sure
For future success…
And happiness…
For…
Too little, too late
Hate will win for sure…*unless love cures*…

Inspiration

Inspiration…
Thought without hesitation
Becomes an emotion…
Expressed thru ideas
Uniqueness…
It does impress…
Imagination…
Not common to us all
Help me to say what lies deep within my soul
It enables the human race
To beautify…
As perfect white lace
Our lives, as dark as they may be
Need rays of light
So we can see
That hope is there
Though briefly it comes
It lights our paths
As does the sun
Gives birth to day
Inspiration…
Highlights our lives,
Enriches us all
As one may see
Art expressed
As a creative force
It does endorse a world of ideas
It fills up the cup
Of emptiness
Numbs the pain at times we feel
A symphony lies within our minds
As silent music heard only to ourselves
Taking us to our paradise…
Though blind our eyes may be
Hidden there within us all…
A masterpiece…

You Can't Stop Love

You can't stop love...
As the wind, it goes where it wishes...
You can't stop love...
Love never needs to replenish
Love runs always full
Never empty
Even when its streams go dry...
Its bountiful source, eternity connected...
Its energy flows from an unseen source...
Love shows itself in many ways...
It speaks often times
Through deeds...
Love reaches out to one's own hurt
Love reaches out even when treated curt
Love opens wide...
Love never hides...
You can't stop love...
Love sees no color
All are equal, one as the other
Love is freely given, not chosen...
Nor selected at random...
Love encompasses the whole
Never neglecting the individual...
Love's emotion quenches anger
Sooths division
Binding all together...
Love has no need to confess
Love is never known
To be remiss...
Love covers all error,
Counters every vice...
Love forgives offenses
Even those committed thrice...
Love respects mankind...
Relationships...
Love is as the iceberg...
One sees only the tip...
But there is still so much more

I'll try to express…
You can't stop love…
It goes on…
Endless…
Love is as the seed unsown…
One can't see what it is
Until it is grown…
Love has potential…
Though it starts out small…
Love is as the cedar..
Steadfast and tall…
Love may be battered
And abused…
Love may at times even be
Killed…
Its emotion may at times be unspoken
But its rays, like the sun, unbent…
Love supports the world
As yet…
And when all is said and done…
You can't stop love…
No, not anyone…

Mistake

I've made a mistake...
Too late...
Too late...
To change the time
No reason...
No rhyme...
Will I yet repeat?
The error I made...in my decision...
My heart did part from reason
For a season, and I'll conclude...
Why didn't I think not once, but twice?...
I had the dice within my hands...
But it's too late,
For until this date...
I've made mistake...
Why did I lie to logic and to reason?
I need some time to think about what I have done...
I have not won this game of chance
For often, it seems that life's a gamble
We place our bet and yet...
We lose...
We lose ourselves...
And all our reason...
For a season...
And why?
We are but human...
We can not help it
We all do draw from weakness at times...
Life is but short, and I'll report
That I, like all the rest,
Have placed my bet, and I think as yet...
That I have lost...
What is the cost?
Is all a failure?...
Maybe so...
But
Begin again...
My friend, my friend...

We all do fall at times in life
You see…
The cost may be great…
But we all make mistakes…
There is this we have in common…
Begin again…
My friend…my friend…
For the mistakes made today…
Yes, we pay…
But then…
Learn from the past; just hold on fast…
To logic and to reason
Tell your heart to quit…
Just get a grip…
You are the wiser now
Begin again…
My friend, my friend
If you can…
Begin again… and again…and again…

You Can't Change What Happens

You can't change what happens...
Come what may...
You can't change what happens...
Even from day to day...
Seasons come; seasons go...
Life follows its own course...
Life, so full of surprises,
Has its victories and reprisals
It directs its winding history...
Acting at times so strangely,
But, *we are all connected*
To each other, you see...
We are all connected
I'll even go so far to say...
Life does not always
Willingly repay...
Sometimes events beyond our control
Surround, hinder, shape and mold
Our future...
Our destiny...
History writes its own story
Don't you see?
We all inherit special gifts, giving merit
To our own worth, of course, to mankind
We all should contribute...
Only then will we glean life's secret...
Destiny...
Does call; it beckons to us all...
Some respond well, but others I'd say...
Expect to be carried...
All life's way...
Some are hurried...their lives are blurry,
Through the cracks, they fall...
And as in the game of dominoes
When one is knocked over...
All the other ones...

Go...
There are those events in life
Of which fate takes hold...
We find confusion, misdirection
We may try at best to follow our dreams...
But dismay covers hope, blankets esteem
We can not see...
Yet this future extends its hand...
Discovery accepts it, accepting a new challenge...
Life's mystery...
Our destiny,
Reveals its truth...
We accept or reject it
We bend; we stand,
For survival compels us all...
Forcing us to kneel to life's balance...
It evens out our lives,
Directs us to what may even perplex us...
While trust steps forward, a new journey to begin...
No,
No one can change what happens...
Try what you will...
You can't change what happens...
Life goes on still...

Intensity

Intensity...
The pressure is on...
From within ourselves...
An uncontrollable force creates of course whatever expression
was meant to be
Intensity...
Can be channeled to benefit mankind
As you will find great masters possessed
Who to some seemed a bit obsessed
Reality, you see...
Became *intensity* to me
Intensity...
Perfection, its driving force...
Held with no remorse to what lengths one may go
Yet, as quiet as the falling snow
Accumulates to monumental status
Intensity...
Influences the mighty
Forcing emotion's reactionary power
To tower, overwhelming most...
Or...
Intensity...
May become a host
Of pleasure...
Without measure, a royal bounty
Far worthy of our admiration
A coronation of ecstasy...
Intensity...
Drives the human race
Beyond our rationale
Intensity
Gives birth to human worth,
Life's creative expression...
There is no lesson to be learned...
Intensity is a gift, never earned...
Accept it with wisdom
To express oneself as far
As limit can go...

To a land far beyond

My Gift

I have something to share...
My gift I have to give...
My soul releasing
All it's been keeping...
Emotion...
Devotion...
It is my turn now...
Melody...
Please come to me...
Open wide the thoughts of my heart...
From deep within...
I will keep within
Secrets from of old...
In time, they will unfold...
For...
Truth, now is speaking...
Over and over repeating...
While conscience is teaching,
What others say...*deny!*
My life that's been tried...
My life that I've lied...
No more silent ache
No more, to let heart break...
Now, I care to give...
Now I share *to live*...
My gift revealed
Yes, life concealed...
Now all that has yearned...
The world will see...
Melancholy,
Be no more!

For the Sake of the Children

For the sake of the children...
Love must abide
For the sake of the children...
Pride and hate must hide
Do away with...
Let go of hold...
For the sake of the children...
Unity must grow
For...
Divided ways have a bitter price to pay
Broken families...
Leave children to waste away
A responsibility abandoned...
Tossed to and fro...
For children do suffer...
Life shows...
For the sake of the children...
What is life all about?
For the sake of the children...
Why argue and shout?
For the sake of the children...
Difference can change
For the sake of the children...
Indifference and independence leaves one's spouse estranged...
For the sake of the children...
Let weakness gain strength
For the sake of the children...
Keep focus, division rends
For the sake of the children...
Don't let greed win
For the sake of the children...
As words unspoken...
Love mends...

Broken Wings

This bird lies broken...
Broken wings can't fly
This bird, love's token...
If left alone...
Will die...
Abused by its enemy
Lurking beneath
A full foliage tree...
Just waiting to pounce...
Heart's kindness
Denounced...
Life's enemy...
Would rather kill,
Than heal...
Do creatures ill
Until...
Now, left alone...
A sad mystery to me...
This bird cries
I hear...
With its silent plea
To me...
It dreams to fly again
Humankind to befriend
From the skies above
This dove...
With music and melody
Will sing...
Though its wing is harmed,
Somehow...
Somehow...
Good will must do
Come safely by
Don't cry...
Don't cry...
Broken wings
Will fly...